THE LITURGICAL DANCER

THE LITURGICAL DANCER

A DANCE OF RAGE, RECONCILIATION, AND RESURRECTION

EDIE LA-CHELLE

ART ILLUSTRATOR COURTNEY VASILIJE

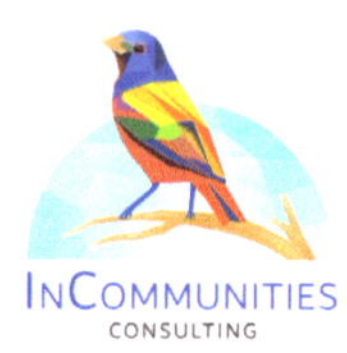

ISBN: 978-1-7362356-0-7 (Print)
ISBN: 978-1-7362356-1-4 (EBook)

Cover and interior book design by Asya Blue
Cover artwork designed by Courtney Vasilije

GRATITUDES

Grateful acknowledgement is made to Courtney Vasilije for your beautiful illustrations and thoughtfulness in turning my words into images that depict my mind, body, heart and soul.

Thank you to the family and friends who were loving enough to hear my stories and help me to embrace my truth.

A special thanks to Reuben Moore for empowering me to be loving, courageous and brave. You gave me a space to see myself and reflect on the beauty that exist within me.

I am extremely grateful to all the Black men who walked away from me because of your willingness to leave me in the pit, I was able to find strength, dignity and integrity to love myself and be ye not afraid to stand on my own two feet.

I am blessed beyond measure for my sweet daughter, Meme La-Chelle, coming into my life when I was ready to throw in the towel on life and love. Your remarkable desire to live has captivated my heart and propelled me forward to live a life totally in love with you and mesmerized by the miraculous power of God.

POETIC CONTENT

PREFACE

At the age of twelve years old, I discovered that I was a fatherless child. While probing into the absence of my father, I learned the details surrounding his untimely death. Simultaneously, I did not feel loved by my mother and the sense of disconnectedness from my mother created bubbling rage in my soul. I felt very alone and vulnerable. Her constant disappearing acts left me predisposed to ongoing molestation from her first cousin, Preacher Boy, between the ages of five and twelve years old.

Without anyone to turn to for help I turned within, and then somewhere deep within myself, I got lost. For more than twenty years I was on a search to find myself, but the more I tried to recover my lost voice, the more I lost direction. I, too, began to experience the loss of loved ones and became further trapped within my own soul. In an attempt to recover my truest self, I learned how to praise dance at church, and then later became an instructor of liturgical dance for children with all abilities.

From 2002–2004, I began to praise dance as a form of praise and worship for national church conferences and higher education institutions throughout Minnesota. This expressive form of sacred dance helped me to reconcile the images of molestation—the sexual abuse committed by my mother's first cousin Preacher Boy—and the intended purpose of my body to carry forth love within a hurting world.

As I experienced personal transformation and healing through liturgical dance, I gained a better understanding of the spiritual power that exists in making and sustaining love. Embracing self-love has created a sense of peace within my mind and soul that has resurrected images of love, joy, and the Divine toward others. Through dance I entered a journey of writing that highlighted recurring themes of my life that shaped my understanding of the world, the local communities I served, and the interconnectedness of church. My writing led to moments of spiritual awakening that resurrected my mind, body, and spiritual being that allowed me to gracefully recount my life experiences into poetic content that liberated my soul from rage and transformed my relationships with others in the form of reconciliation that all for my vision for creating a sustainable ministry to experience resurrection.

INTRODUCTION

The Dance of Rage is an exploration of the dynamics of grief and intrapsychic loss from sad, hurtful interactions with black men experiencing premature sexual intimacy. Some of the poetic content creates images of homelessness and displacement for women who do not give voice to their pain and hurt as they find themselves evicted from their own sense of joy, peace, and self-love. The dark cloud of confusion hovers around their minds, bodies, and spirits, the fact of which displaces them from their authentic self in their relationships and in society.

The Dance of Reconciliation is a two-part dance between themes of love and forgiveness. In my early years, I discovered reconciliation was one of the seven sacraments of the Catholic faith. The Roman Catholic Church identified seven sacraments (which means "a sign of the sacred" from the Latin word *sacramentum*) that are holy ceremonies that point to what is sacred, significant, and important for Christians. They are special occasions for experiencing God's saving presence that can be instruments of God's grace. In the Catholic tradition, reconciliation has three elements—conversion, confession, and celebration—that allow us to accept God's unconditional forgiveness as we are called to forgive others. I truly learned how to embrace the power and meaning of reconciliation by way of relinquishing my daily fears and learning to trust myself in loving others, forgiving myself, and living in each moment so I could experience the humanness of life, love, death, or economic hardship without any guilt or shame.

The Dance of Resurrection is a transformative process of surrendering to a greater Divine power through prayer and praise to live a fully awakened life. I have experienced a sense of love and compassion in the face of sadness. Through will and determination, I seek to continuously embrace the power of love and interconnectedness with humankind. In this phase of life, I find myself experiencing balance between the knowledge of wisdom, goodness, and happiness and the actualization of these things in the fulfillment of purpose.

THE DANCE OF RAGE

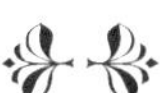

A Dark Cloud In Hell

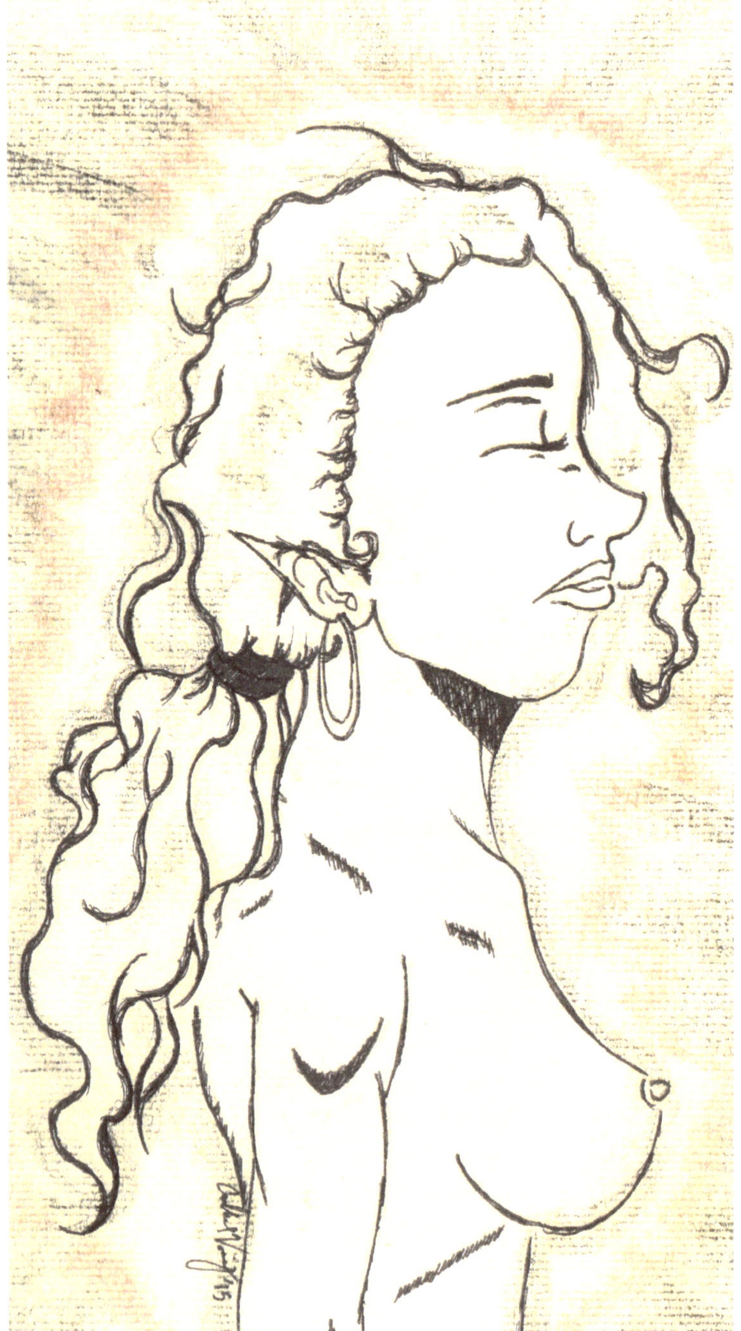

ADDICTION (A-DICK-SHUN)

He didn't even call yet.
My phone is silent.
I can hear the wind.

He asked me, "What's
wrong?"
Timing.
I can't tell you over
the phone.
Dead silence.

My tears well up in
my mind.
I hear God's
calls for help,
but I ignore the pain.

My God, I am lonely
And hurt beyond measure.
But He didn't even notice
the wounds and scars left.

Feenin' for love and intimacy
At whatever the cost. I trade
In my soul for a quick three seconds
Then right back, longing for love.

Fornication has become a replacement
For true love and intimacy, but at least
I can count on It to be there.
All I have to do is moan loud and It answers.

Yet still, something is steady missing,
But fornication is quick and cheap,
So, I pay for him to come and go as I please,
Stealing total control over me!

THE STORY OF BLACK LUCIFER

Black Lucifer,
Disguised as Jesus Christ, a lover of peace
Only long enough to sex me
And drive me to insanity.
All the promises that you made, long enough
To get me laid, soon to be broken.

After I told you no over and over again,
You barged into my heart and ripped my love
Out again, and tore it into three pieces:
Despair, distress and discouragement.
As I cried out please no more stop please stop
You pulled out to stop penetrating me, then dropped me,
Bleeding and crying on the bathroom floor.

As I fell to the floor, bleeding in my own tears,
Crying out please Lord God stop the pain and the fear,
I wish I did not fear the man who abused me;
Abused my love, my sweet, sweet love
To have control over me.
In the words of Langston Hughes,
In winter I am the broken-winged bird
That cannot fly.

Positioned north, with a noose around my neck,
I am in a hole of passion and pain
That no man can pull me out of.
You, that has dug a hole in my soul so deep
You have left me confused and weak.

Black Lucifer
Shattered my soul and left my whole world cold;
Stole my heart and left my mind scattered,
Rejected my inner being, and left me disembodied,
Oppressed my body and left me captive by insanity.
Real love is accepting not rejecting, leaving my soul,
Bleeding fears internally.
I cannot move
I cannot move.

After I told you to leave and never return,
You returned and stripped away my identity,
Leaving doubt to fester inside of me.
Disappointment follows me, and loves
to live outside of me,
Love waiting to sneak up on me, but
Self hatred lurks around my neck.

Suicide convicted and committed me.

GREETINGS DEATH,

Tears strolling down my face
Memories of you cannot be erased
Leaving my heart bleeding in pain
Living my life there's nothing to gain
But still emotions of dying remain
locked inside of me
who in the hell stole my soulful butterfly
both tears and fears drive me insane
why did my grandma have to die in vain

I ask myself this when nothing or no one is left
Why didn't God trade me for her;
living here alone often troubles me
Why wasn't Death asking for my hand in the dance of life
instead,
Death crept upon her heart
while stirring her first big pot of gumbo

I suppose God still has plenty of work
to complete within me
I suppose God felt a need to let her return
to ashes and dust since she spent her life
loving, praying and saving me

Well done, Grandma! You were a servant
Of love, fulfillment, humor, and tender care
I suppose the task of Death still could not
keep you from living freely within me as
envisioned memories of you are far stronger
than death.

MALCOLM'S VISION,
A TRIBUTE TO FIREMEN

When I look in his eyes
I see myself:
Broken, hurt, confused

When I look in his eyes
I see my mistakes
In letting love slip away

When I look in his eyes
I see a painful reflection
Of my soul

Together we look intensely
Into each other's eyes
And the more I see into
His soul,
I cannot hold the pain in
So, I cry

Lord why did you bring
Two broken-winged birds
Together to confuse and
Inflict each other

God replied, "To give you strength from
his healed wing and to give him
protection within your love!"

When I hear his words
I hear the tragedy
Of my life story

When I hug him
I feel a shielded heart
Crumble, it is mine too

Together we mirror each
Other's hurts, joys,
seizing moments of
Opportunities,
So, I smile

Divine God, thank you
for such a healing love.

THE CRY OF A POWERLESS WOMAN

A woman lying on a park bench
With dingy brown clothes
and stringy blonde hair
Reeking of a three-year odor from
divorce from water, food, and shelter

A woman standing alone
surrounded
by a circle of dull stars
Pointing her finger to the east
And as I followed her fingertip
There was nothing there.

No Power to Ask, No Power to Choose

A woman who cries within and sits mute
Gazing at invisible things
She shuts down
Outside these four walls
Staring into daydreams never revealing
any truths
her mortal body dies, returning her dreams
and goals back to Heaven
while her soul still roams the earth

No Power to Ask, No Power to Choose

THE VOICELESS CRY

The voiceless child with an enormous cry
yelling to the top of her lungs
for her mommy,
"Please don't leave me!"

After her mommy leaves
she closes herself up in the coat closet
Sitting on the coldness of hardwood floors
between hanging tagged cleanser's clothes
and old, dingy winter coats—
she clings to scents of moth balls and pine sol.

As she continues to cry, her little pudgy brother
opens the door to see tears streaming down
her face, long as the Nile River.
He reaches out his hand to console her.

As he lifts her up, he says, "What are you crying for?
She'll be right back. I promise. Come out the closet
and eat some ice cream with me."
She cries, "I don't want any ice cream
I just want my momma."

The voiceless child huffed and puffed in efforts to
stop the endless tears releasing from her
broken heart and troubled soul.
With limited faith in her mother's return
depression emerged.

Two hours later, the phone rings and
the little girl answers: "Mommy caught a
one-way train to Canada to start a new life!"

The voiceless child knew she'd never return.
Twenty-five years later, the little girl is still
living in the closet and refuses to come out.

As an ally of the LGBTQ community, I dedicate this poem to
all men, women, and children who are afraid to love the person
they choose throughout childhood and adulthood. This is also
dedicated to my family and friends who belong to the LGBTQ
community; a prayer of hope for you to truly and sincerely be
who you are.

WHAT WOULD YOU DO?

What would you do if your life
Was full of pain? Nothing to gain.
Would you ask for medication or
Simply Endure?

What would you do if your soulmate
Cheated on you? No one to comfort.
Would you ask for a hitman or
Simply Forgive?

What would you do if my story of rape
Was your story too? No one believes you.
Would you retaliate, or in prayer,
Simply Petition?

What would you do if you had no food
to eat and yo' momma ran the streets?
Would you believe in Jesus or James, the
Neighborhood drug dealer who fed you?

What would you do if you had no friends
To talk to, no one is listening—not even Jesus?
Would you call the police for attention or
Hold a gun on your classmates in detention?

What would you do if God disowned you,
Would you dig your own grave,
Disappearing off the face of the Earth
Or shoot yourself in the head—
Short-lived, vegetable, dead?

THE DANCE OF RECONCILITATION

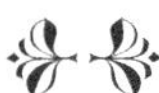

Awakening from Darkness

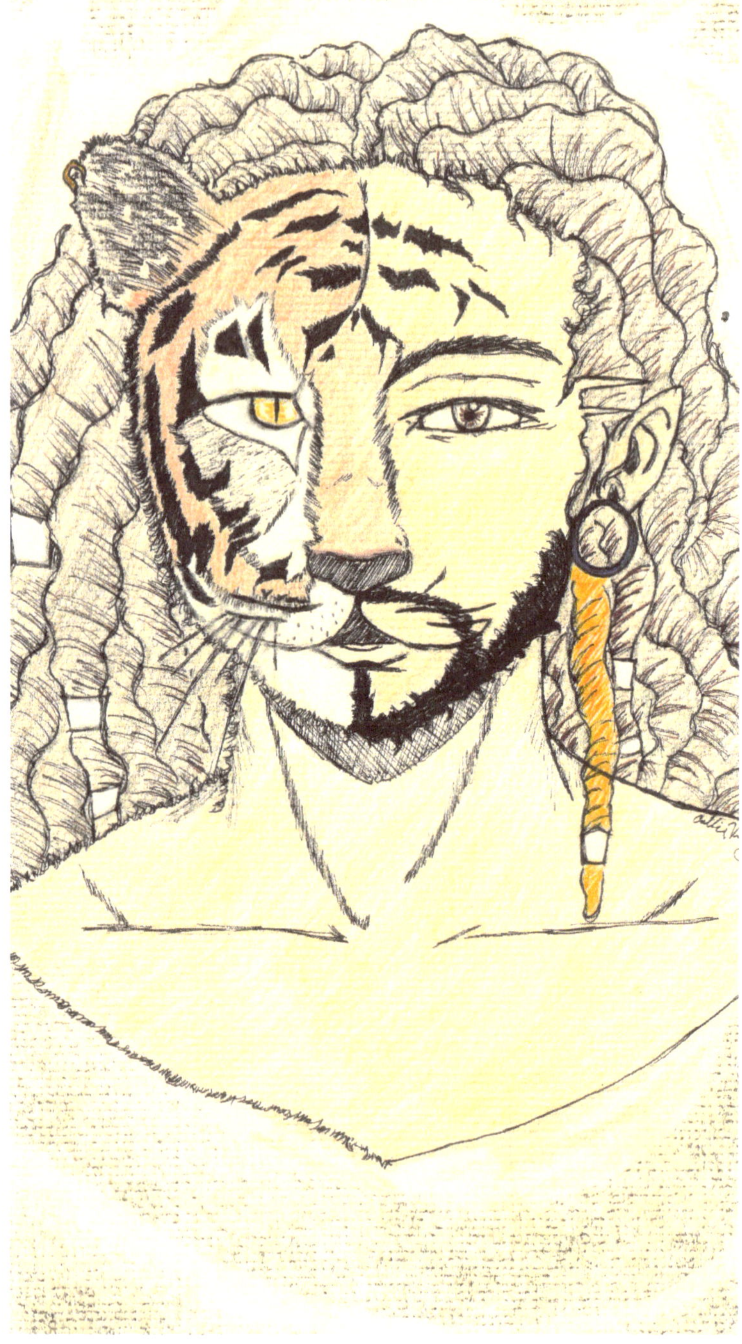

COLORS OF LIFE

My life is like
when a child color
The child never ponders the color to choose
She just scribbles with all the colors from the box,
she colors outside the lines
Without contemplation,
she simply starts
the process of coloring

Like my life I thoughtlessly choose
People, places, and things to take up
Space in my heart; never contemplating
The long-term effect of those choices
On my life from a distance

When I see the colors chosen,
I affirm the child
Her picture may turn out beautifully
Then she chooses to continue to color
With the same bright orange and ruby red
crayons until they become dull
I ask, "Why not explore two other colors?"
A change of colors may destroy
my display of art, my perfect image

When I turn inwardly to look deeper
Oh, how I see the poignant similarities
Of her coloring and my living—
Never from the box but most certainly outside the lines
I see the disaster of my life
Fatherless was never imagined from coloring with
shades of gray

In that moment I stop to change
But with the same people, places and things
Surrounding me
"What's the sense of changing colors?"

My life soon will come to an end
Which portrait looks better my life or the one that I colored?

When the Divine God reminds us of the integrative process of Mind, Body and Soul and Spirit. We allow the intangible forces of love to reconcile our minds to our hearts. We enter the sacred space of:

Reconciliation: rec·on·cil·i·a·tion
/ˌrekənˌsilēˈāSH(ə)n/

The act of bringing together thought with action. The process of acknowledging the interconnectedness of theory and practice. The warm embrace of discourse and harmony for nurturing ourselves and the world around us.

Words from my heart and soul
Edie La-Chelle

IMPRESSIONS

Impressions marvel

thy soul to wonder whose heart

is real or fake?

LIVING IN THE MOMENT

In this moment we share
Our innermost thoughts
About war, family, death
Death vs. dying
It's like life without living

In this moment we stare
In each other's eyes
To witness simple purity
Pure vs. white
It's like making love without sex

In this moment we scatter
Our hearts
In random surface conversations
Never do our minds really meet

In this moment we hear
Our deepest prayers
As the music plays over and over again
As you abandon the church pew
In front of me to sit beside me

In this moment we see
Inner and outer beauty
As our souls meet and connect
Beyond our human understanding

In this moment we touch
The cup of java
As our hands embrace
My skin tone turns from white to gray
As I imagine being a white man's Queen

In this moment we breathe
The thin air
As our bodies nestle in the chairs
Afraid to let more than our conversations meet

In this moment we feel
Our fears rise upward
About love, lies, commitment & politics
Is interracial dating even still in?

In this moment we chant
Our worldviews
About life's injustices

By the end of the conversation
We find ourselves in a new recession
In this moment we experience
Hypocrisy
About who we truly are
Because if we reveal who we are
Then we will find ourselves passionately in love
Dismissing fear from her final resting place

A WOMAN'S INTUITION

Within you there is a small bronze statue
painted very low within your soul
"It" is finely twisted up inside of you,
some may refer to it as your intestines,
but as it rises slowly upward to the north
for what is right, just, and good
it gives you inner peace and courage to be
who you are and to do what you believe.

"It" gives you wings to soar up like
an eagle when life's journey gets you down
it takes you high above ground when your
foundation has been laid on rocks of love,
it gives you hope to trust the God in you
despite all the pain faced at ground zero.

The statue inside is not a physical part of
your body but a mystery of hope within
your soul, waiting to emerge
it creates strength and power in your mind
and your heart to move you forward
when no one or nothing can.

But, if you move too quickly or not quick
enough you just might miss it,
that "It" is called A Woman's Intuition.

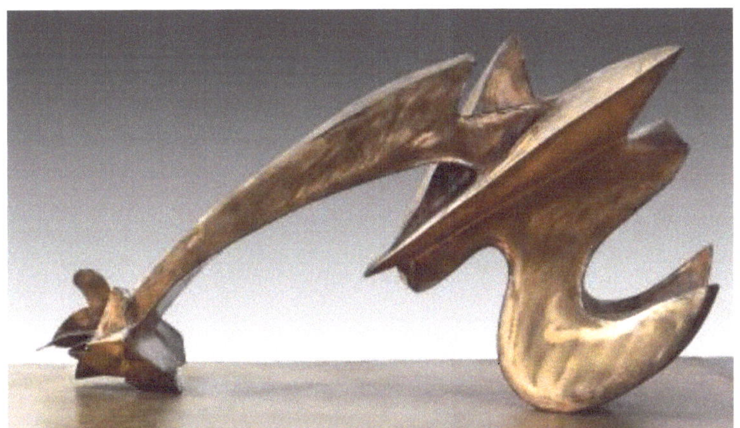

Inspired by Richard Hunt's Touring Exhibition

The Museum of African American History, Detroit, Michigan

Sculptor Richard Hunt was born September 12, 1935, on Chicago's historic South Side. I developed a fondness of Mr. Hunt's work in 2003. I am deeply inspired by the abstract shapes that gives rise to my feelings of the known and unknown.

Mr. Hunt and I have a love for okra. I believe those of us who love the taste of okra whether it is mixed within a pot of gumbo or fried in a cast iron skill we possess like Mr. Hunt a love for compassionate social justice and a deep commitment to civil rights. My soul loves Mr. Hunt's work, artistic brilliance and humble beginnings. I share a spiritual bond with Mr. Hunt through an ability to transform raw material with space into a unified field of communal love, courage and social responsibility.

I am extremely grateful to Mr. Hunt's work that displayed at The Museum of African American History in my hometown Detroit, Michigan. Witnessing his work sparked a story within my soul to celebrate women and honor the strong women who birth brave and amazingly talented men.

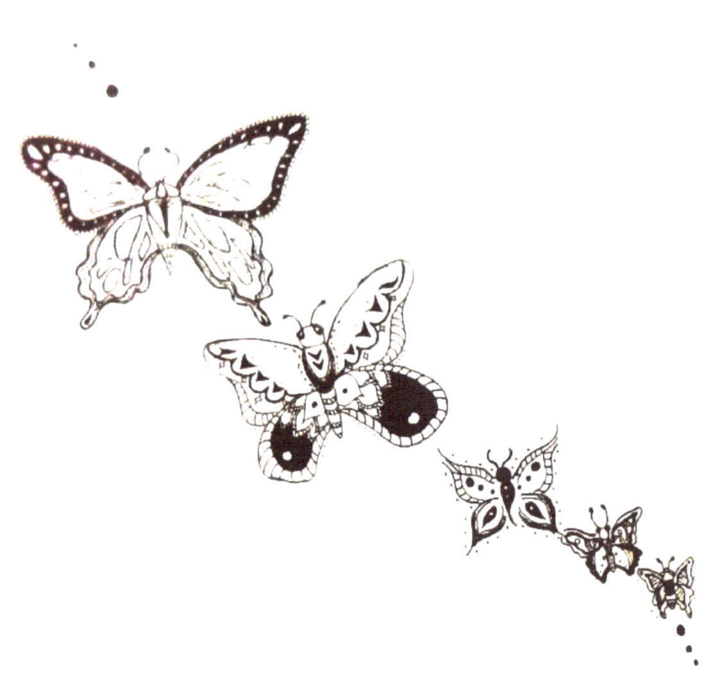

A TRIBUTE TO MY MATRIARCH BUTTERFLIES

Grandma Edie Wallace (4/26/41–1/26/10)
Great Aunt Mildred Hall Caldwell (11/20/39–2/4/12)
Auntie Yvonne Borden (9/10/56–9/11/12)
Great Cousin Lisa Ann Wallace (3/8/67–5/27/03)
Great Cousin Denise Hall (6/23/57–4/25/11)

My Sweet, Loving First Cousin Kennetta Marie Borden
(9/16/74–4/12/17)

A small brown creature
with four large wings of
compassion, courage,
love, strength

Her soft brown wings
Spread with delicate
Beauty, honesty, integrity, loyalty, and joy

It was your wings of compassion
That I remember most,
The unconditional love
you showed to my mother when she refused to
Return your call,
You forgave her as I constantly struggle to do

Her distinctive mouthpart
Feeds wisdom of life to
Family, strangers, and friends

It was your wings of love
That I hold onto
knowing you fed me
The very last serving of food
When you had no food
To feed yourself

In all your sweetness,
You nurture us to spring
Forth petals of love with
Stems of strength
Her nature of beauty
Showers gardens of familial ties to bloom in peace

It was your wings of courage
That I believe
Kept you here on Earth with us
Long enough to testify to
God's power in creating possibilities

We are the flowers,
You are the Butterfly,
You feed from us and
We grow from you.
While at rest you continue
to hold your wings upright
to God,
basking in all God's glory
I celebrate you.

It was your wings of strength
That I will truly miss
As I pray to embody strength
To carry your light throughout
Our family and the world,
I promise to remember you, Lady Butterfly.

A small brown creature
That feeds off the nutrients
Of our souls as you enter
The fullness of God's mold!

MY TRUEST DWELLING PLACE

In the comfort of God's arms,
My heart and my head lay
In God's hands.
I rest, embodied in
My truest dwelling place.

Laying in God's arms,
My heart and my soul often sing
Beautiful praises and hymns.
I worship, living in
My truest dwelling place.

Resting in God's arms,
My heart and my head often imagine
Flowing waters and streams.
I float, onward in
My truest dwelling place.

As God's angelic spirit cheers
My heart and my ears hear God's voice,
Uttering, "Welcome home my child.
Welcome to the comfort of My arms,
Your truest dwelling place."

Trusting in God's love and grace,
My heartfelt prayers illuminate my soul
With faith and peace on this journey.
I found my truest dwelling place
exists within me.

BLESS PHILO-SOPHIA

In the beginning the God of love created
a Black Woman from strong roots of
purple lilies

The soul of the Black Woman continuously
prayed and sought the God of love
morning, noon, and night for mass
reproduction and to grow a nation

She whispered in the wind
The Black Woman fell into a deep sleep
The God of love blew Her Spirit
Onto the Black Woman's womb
To conceive the image of a
Strong Black Man

As the Black Woman awoke,
the Black Man appeared,
standing Tall with instructions
in His right hand

The scroll read, "Explore life with this
Woman, do not leave her side or forsake
Her trust, build a life together worthy
Of my love and praise."
The two unnamed stumbled through
Unpaved roads, uninhabited land
To construct a vision of love, power,
And wisdom for the sake of
waging pleasure in the midst of
regrettable pain.

The God of love stretched Her staff
Toward the two unnamed with an ounce
Of Her power naming Black Man, Philo,
the Greek god of power and Black Woman,
Sophia, the Greek goddess of wisdom

Philo and Sophia intertwined their power
and wisdom to brccd a nation of knowledge
Philosophy produced a theology of love,
Music, politics, law

THE DANCE OF RESURRECTION

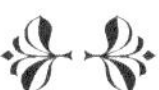

Love's *Sweet Embrace*

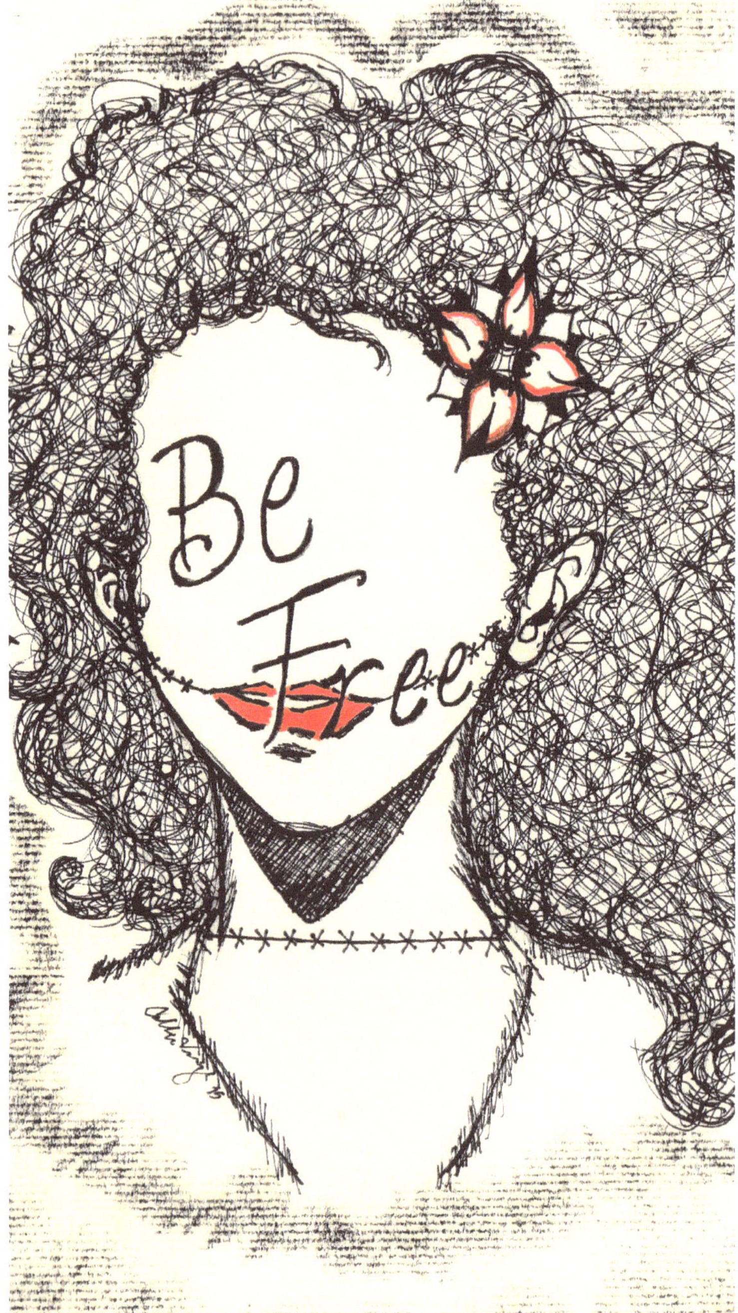

Be
Free

A PRAYER FOR ESPERANZA'S HOPE

Dream, Esperanza,
dream again
when someone rapes you,
rapes you of your dreams

Be free, Esperanza,
Seek freedom
when someone robs you,
robs you of your civil rights

Receive your blessings, Esperanza,
Open your hand to accept abundance
when someone steals from you,
steals from your bleeding heart

Live, laugh, and hope, Esperanza,
Embrace empowerment
When someone breaks your spirit,
breaking your spirit, they cannot do

Esperanza, you are rich in love, beauty
Purple and angelic in nature, when the
Time comes you will see you are royalty

A LOVE LETTER TO MY FRIEND

My dear friend,
Friendships are sacred because
Of the tender love given and the
Gentle invitation of intertwining
Spirits, whether in pure conversation
Or discontented dialogue.

Friends calm the raging storms of life,
Bring aid to pain, whether its pain
From a miserable breakup or a
Past childhood hurt, friends know how
To soothe one's soul.

You, my friend, at some point or another,
Have given me hope to move onward,
To appreciate my strides onto a journey
Of uncertainty and compassion.

No longer will I cry tears of agony, defeat
I will embrace my past life, holding onto
An unpredictable future, all the while living in
This moment, remembering you, a friend of
Goodness, compassion, and truth. You remind
Me of God: divine, gentle, faithful, and true.

You were a friend I lost touch with, yet
Only for a moment I had completely forgotten
your fragrance and the scent that once lingered
in my heart, but in this moment of sullen tears and
insanity, my recollection of us praise dancing
together gives peace to my heart.

Or studying for a test I've yet to pass, but
in this moment
Our lives cross paths again and I don't want to regret
Another moment lost, so slow down, wait, let us take
This picture together to savory this moment.

How can that be possible since we both live so very far,
You're there in Heaven and I'm here on Earth,
My ancestral line of African and Native American teaches Me
to believe that you exist
in Spirit and Truth,
You exist in the budding roses of my Grandfather Al's garden,
you exist
in the center of my daughter's soul, you exist
as I stand in the pulpit giving my first sermon, you exist when
the Sun kisses the moon, you exist,
you truly exist in my Heart too.

IN MY DAUGHTER'S EYES
MY TRIBUTE TO DEMETRIA

A Sweet Soul with Trisomy 18

I never knew how important vision was
until you had trouble looking at me
Often I took for granted the world
That you would see

Now I realize that you will never
View the world like me
Simple walks in the park or strolls in the zoo
Are difficult yet we still enjoy the times shared

I imagine you visualize in your mind
The world as a loving place
From the sound of the sweet songs
That I sing you to sleep

Without words there is no way for me to truly know

Your grip around my neck and
Sweet embrace tells my soul
That love, peace, and gentleness
Lurks around your heart

Your smile is my daily affirmation
That I'm doing a great job parenting you
Greatness and big dreams I still hold for you

Stares into each other's eyes on long lonely nights
Has kept me from crying as Your Eyes sing
my soul alive.

SILVER SPIRIT

inspired by 1980 Rolls Royce

By sight: crisp, flawless style;
Shined to the T, in tip-top shape
His movement is classic; slow in motion
And breathtaking

When he speaks, I stop to listen and
Crowds draw near to hear
The wisdom of a king spoken
With an old man's swag

My sweet honey dip's platinum love
Cannot be auctioned on eBay
Or advertised on Craigslist

I am a mere reflection of everything
He is and hopes to be

His silver spirit is highly rated next to
Gold
As we both know God carries
The most fortune and wealth untold

Riding high from the plateau of Nevada to the most
Lowly places in Michigan
His passion travels the distance
In love he comes and when he comes
We cruise into the morning sunset

A new day, a new journey we embark upon
We both acknowledge and thank God
For our newfound love, an adventure
in my spirit of knowing he was fashioned for me
By my faith in God I trust that God saved,
At last, this one King (has risen)
With his silver lining spirit just for me!

A RESURRECTED LOVE

God's spirit blew over
desolate, depressed, and destroyed
places.

At midnight
my dead, dry love life
inhaled breath,
exhaled limited thinking,
immature ways, and
confused moments.

At 2 a.m.,
my love life has
been fully restored
because of two people's
faith in love and in the
God of love,
restorative love, and healing
prevailed.

At 4 a.m.,
the man of my life
makes passionate, sensual,
and intense love to me.
Orgasm after orgasm; excitement
of intense lovemaking fills the air.

God's spirit and love manifests
Intensely as our horny little bodies
Gyrate in circular motion.

At 6 a.m.,
my mind, body, and soul whispers
gently a language of love; acts of service
a language only your soul deciphers
from distant peaks of sexuality
with images of marriage
dancing the night away
in our crowns as we slowly
drift into a blissful sleep.

TO A LOVE UNKNOWN

Your love lightens up
Every room of my thoughts.
From astrology to zymology,
Degrees of ecstasy enter my soul.

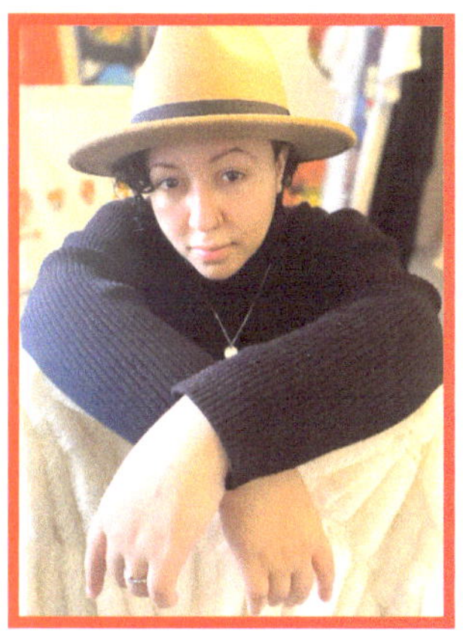

Self taught artist from Detroit, Courtney Vasilije, thrives from creating art that touches the community. You can find her art pieces on Instagram @vasilije_the_art_goddess

EPILOGUE

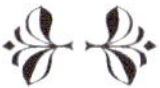

In the words of the late beloved, prolific Prophet Ermias "Nipsey Hussle" Asghedom, "the highest human act is to inspire." I pray the poetic content in this book will inspire women and girls to speak their truth and never cower in the face of painful sins committed against you. Be ye not dismay from the trauma or residual trauma that exists as you journey through life. Know that nothing is missing from you nor does anything need to be fixed within you. Please learn from me and do not waste 30 years trying to fix yourself to be perfect because perfection does not exist in you or the people you are seeking to be perfect for. Use your life as a testimony of faith, joy and beauty to inspire the next generation of women and girls to thrive beyond their current circumstances.

Thank you for taking the time to journey through snippets of my life. May peace and contentment find you and you listen to your soul to create a life that is worth living from your place of wholeness.

Peace, love and light,

Edie La-Chelle